United States
Department of
Agriculture

Forest Service

Southern
Research Station

Resource Bulletin
SRS–163

# Virginia Harvest and Utilization Study, 2007

James W. Bentley and
Tony G. Johnson

## The Authors:

**James W. Bentley**, Resource Forester, and **Tony G. Johnson**, Resource Analyst, U.S. Forest Service, Southern Research Station, Knoxville, TN 37919.

September 2009

Southern Research Station
200 W.T. Weaver Blvd.
Asheville, NC 28804

## Foreword

This resource bulletin describes the principal findings of a harvest and utilization study conducted during the eighth inventory of Virginia's forest resources. Survey crews sampled and measured trees harvested in a variety of logging operations, and analysts calculated wood volume and percent of wood utilization. Harvest volume data and factors for growing-stock and nongrowing-stock logging residue are described and interpreted.

Annual surveys of America's forest resources are mandated by the Forest and Rangeland Act of 1978. Surveys and utilization studies are part of a continuing, nationwide undertaking by regional experiment stations of the Forest Service, U.S. Department of Agriculture. Inventories and utilization studies of the 13 Southern States (Alabama, Arkansas, Florida, Georgia, Kentucky, Louisiana, Mississippi, North Carolina, Oklahoma, South Carolina, Tennessee, Texas, and Virginia), the Commonwealth of Puerto Rico, and the U.S. Virgin Islands are conducted by the Southern Research Station, Forest Inventory and Analysis (FIA) Research Work Unit. Unit headquarters is in Knoxville, TN, and FIA has operational offices in Asheville, NC, and Starkville, MS. The primary objective of these appraisals is to develop and maintain resource information needed to formulate sound forest policies and programs. More information about Forest Service resource inventories

is available in "The Enhanced Forest Inventory and Analysis Program—National Sampling Design and Estimation Procedures" (Bechtold and Patterson 2005).

Tabular data included in FIA resource bulletins present a comprehensive array of forest resource statistics, but additional information is available to those who require more specific information. Access to data for the Southern States can be found at: http://srsfia2.fs.fed.us/data/index.shtml.

## Acknowledgments

The authors thank John Pemberton and John Ignosh for their review and comments; Anne Jenkins, Carolyn Steppleton, Janet Griffin, and Sharon Johnson for the map, tables, graphs, and statistical checking; and the Southern Research Station (SRS) Technical Publications Team for editorial review, styling, and publication of this report.

The SRS gratefully acknowledges the cooperation and assistance of the Virginia Department of Forestry in collecting harvest and utilization data. Appreciation is also extended to forest industry and loggers for allowing access to their land and logging operations.

# Contents

[a] All tables in this report are available in Microsoft® Excel workbook files. Upon request, these files will be supplied in the format the customer requests.

The use of trade or firm names in this publication is for reader information and does not imply endorsement by the U.S. Department of Agriculture of any product or service.

Figure 1—Harvest operations, Virginia, 2007.

# Virginia Harvest and Utilization Study, 2007

## James W. Bentley and Tony G. Johnson

## Introduction

Forest planners and managers have a continuing need for information about the timber resource, and the general public is expressing increasing interest in the effects of logging. Therefore, up-to-date data on the Nation's forests—and how the forests are changing—are essential to well-informed decisionmaking. Information about the condition of and changes in the timber resource of Virginia comes from three primary sources: (1) inventory plots, which describe current conditions and quantify changes due to mortality, growth, removals, and land use; (2) mill surveys, which quantify timber volume harvested and delivered to primary wood products facilities, i.e., sawmills, pulpmills, veneer mills, composite panel mills, and pole mills; and (3) logging utilization studies, which characterize harvest operations and quantify the timber volume that is cut and utilized, and that portion that is left in the forest.

This bulletin presents the findings of a 2007 harvest and utilization study in Virginia. The study's main goal was to provide an estimate of softwood and hardwood volume used, and of volume left in the woods as logging residue. Survey crews randomly selected and measured felled trees on 81 active harvest operations throughout Virginia (fig. 1). This bulletin also provides information on logging in Virginia and some general characteristics of trees harvested for various products, examples of which are average diameter at breast height (d.b.h.) by product, average bole length by product, average heights of residual stumps, and average diameter outside bark (d.o.b.) at the end of utilization.

Some standard Forest Inventory and Analysis (FIA) terms are used in this study. Two FIA terms of particular importance in understanding and interpreting study results are growing stock and nongrowing stock. A growing-stock tree is a live tree of commercial species that either contains or is capable of producing at least one 12-foot or two 8-foot logs in the saw-log portion of the bole. A nongrowing-stock tree is one that does not meet the requirements of growing stock due to poor form or rot. For growing-stock trees, the growing-stock portion of a tree (5-inches d.b.h. or larger) includes the volume of sound wood between a 1-foot stump and a 4-inch top, d.o.b. Volume in the 1-foot stump, volume in the main stem from 4 inches to the growing top of the tree, and the volume of any limbs 4 inches or larger with at least one 5-foot section are considered nongrowing-stock

volume by FIA standards. Rough or rotten trees were also sampled and make up another piece of nongrowing-stock (cull) volume. Figure 2 illustrates a poletimber and a sawtimber tree and the growing-stock section of each.

## Methods

### Site Stratification and Selection

Producing a complete list of timber-harvesting operations and ownerships in a region such as Virginia is problematic. Because of the complexity of the timber industry, it is impossible to list the names and locations of all harvesting operations under way during the timeframe considered in this resource bulletin. Many uncontrollable factors affect how, when, and where harvesting operations take place, but the most common events that affect harvesting operations are weather and timber markets. A random sample provides a reasonably accurate estimate of utilization.

The sites selected for study were stratified by species group and product according to the most recent data available on county-level output of timber products harvested in Virginia by species group (Howell and Becker 2006). Using those proportions, we designated 41 of the 81 selected sites as softwood operations, and the remaining 40 as hardwood operations. We used the same guidelines to designate harvest operations by product but allowed more flexibility because of the difficulty in locating harvesting operations for some specific products. Table 1 shows the final breakdown number of harvest operations, total trees, trees planted, and percentage of trees planted by product and species group.

After the harvest operations were stratified by major species group and product, the operations were placed in the appropriate region and county in the State. Using county-level product output data from the "Virginia's Timber Industry—An Assessment of Timber Product Output and Use, 2003" (Howell and Becker 2006) and a map that showed current mill locations, prospective utilization sites were selected based on a high probability of being able to locate a harvesting operation for the particular product and species group assigned. Figure 1 shows where the final harvest operations considered in this bulletin were located.

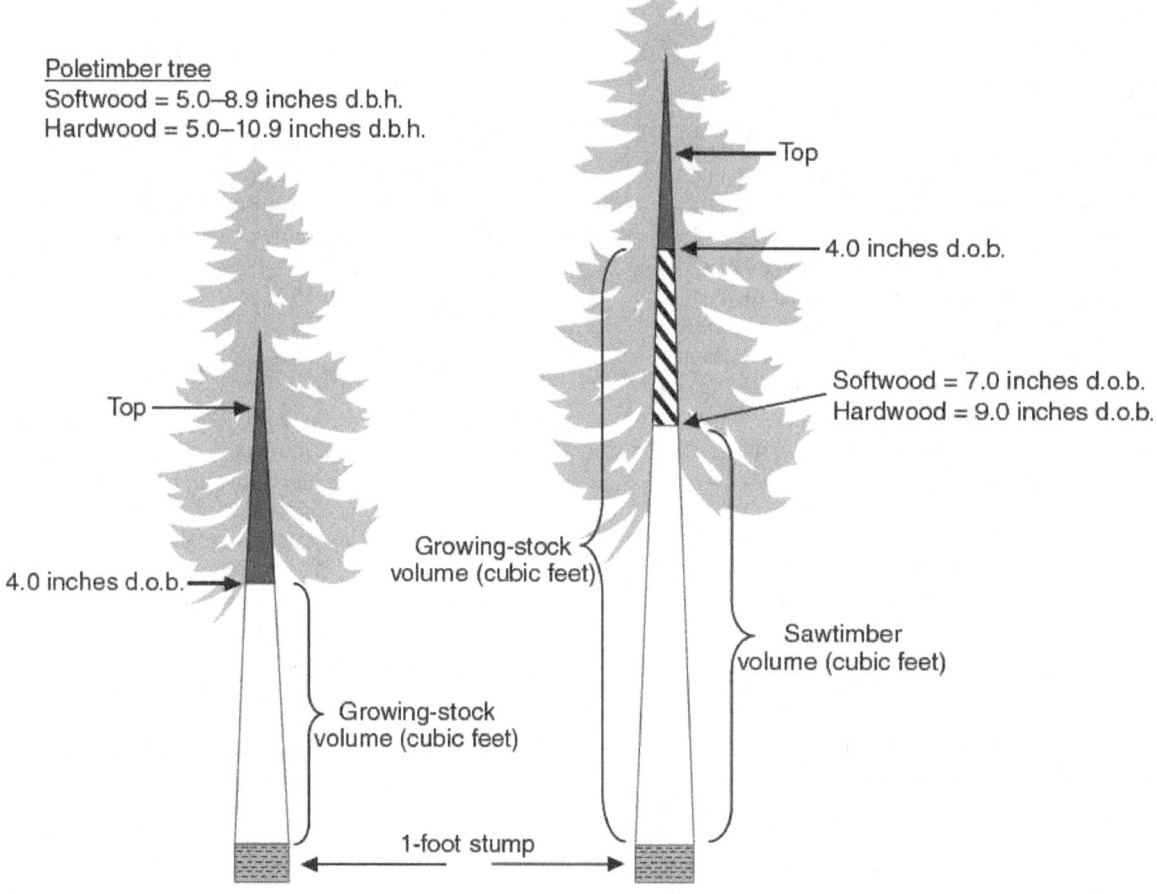

Poletimber tree
Softwood = 5.0–8.9 inches d.b.h.
Hardwood = 5.0–10.9 inches d.b.h.

Sawtimber tree
Softwood = at least 9.0 inches d.b.h.
Hardwood = at least 11.0 inches d.b.h.

Top

4.0 inches d.o.b.

Softwood = 7.0 inches d.o.b.
Hardwood = 9.0 inches d.o.b.

Top

4.0 inches d.o.b.

Growing-stock volume (cubic feet)

Sawtimber volume (cubic feet)

Growing-stock volume (cubic feet)

1-foot stump

Figure 2—Stem sections of poletimber and sawtimber trees.

## Data Collection

In May 2007, field crews were trained to collect data on felled trees at harvest locations. Using the list of operations and a map of sites, they began collecting data by county for the particular species group and designated product(s). From May 2007 to March 2008, field crews collected data on active harvest operations. To locate active harvest sites, field crews visited local mills and consulted with county personnel.

At each harvest operation site, field crews talked to the logger or the person in charge of operations. These contacts provided vital information about product(s) utilized,

specific diameters, and log lengths the receiving mill(s) would accept, along with minimum diameters at the cutoff points for specific products. Field crews also noted the type of logging equipment used. This information was used to determine the level of mechanization involved in each harvesting operation.

On each harvest operation site, the goal of the field crew was to measure 25 to 30 trees for each product. This number ensured an adequate representation of overutilization and underutilization for a given type of harvest operation. Trees were randomly selected and had to be at least 5 inches d.b.h. and alive prior to harvest. Although they often had been bucked, limbed, and topped, the main bole of each tree

**Table 1—Number of operations, total trees, planted trees, and percent planted by product and species group, Virginia, 2007**

| Product and species group | Operations | Trees Total | Planted | |
|---|---|---|---|---|
| | | - - - - - - - *number* - - - - - - - | | *percent* |
| Saw logs | | | | |
| Softwood | 18 | 459 | 251 | 55 |
| Hardwood | 19 | 401 | 1 | 0 |
| Total | 37 | 860 | 252 | 29 |
| Composite panels | | | | |
| Softwood | 7 | 155 | 106 | 68 |
| Hardwood | 3 | 78 | 6 | 8 |
| Total | 10 | 233 | 112 | 48 |
| Pulpwood | | | | |
| Softwood | 16 | 472 | 298 | 63 |
| Hardwood | 15 | 373 | 71 | 19 |
| Total | 31 | 845 | 369 | 44 |
| Fuelwood | | | | |
| Softwood | 0 | 0 | 0 | — |
| Hardwood | 3 | 78 | 0 | — |
| Total | 3 | 78 | 0 | — |
| All products | | | | |
| Softwood | 41 | 1,086 | 655 | 60 |
| Hardwood | 40 | 930 | 78 | 8 |
| Total | 81 | 2,016 | 733 | 36 |

— = no sample for the cell.

selected for measurement had to be intact to be measured for utilization. The State, unit, county, and location number were recorded for each site. Each tree was assigned a number and identified by species, d.b.h., tree class, product, bole length, and percentage of cull (if rot was detected). Each tree was measured from the top of the cut stump to the end of utilization. Measurements were made along the main stem in sections no longer than 16 feet until the end of utilization. The end of utilization usually is determined by the sawyer, according to particular specifications set by the receiving mill(s). FIA merchantability standards for growing-stock volume are defined as the volume in the main stem of the tree from a 1-foot stump to a 4-inch top. However, most trees are not cut exactly at a 1-foot stump, nor are they cut off at exactly 4 inches. For example, trees cut off above a 1-foot stump and below 4 inches would be considered underutilized, and that volume not utilized would be considered growing-stock residue. On the other hand, by FIA standards, trees cut below a 1-foot stump and above a 4-inch top are considered 100-percent utilized, and those portions below and above are considered overutilization. A myriad of combinations actually occurs on active harvest operations. The aggregated volume from measured trees has provided overutilization and underutilization factors that can be applied to statewide inventory results for an estimate of growing-stock and nongrowing-stock logging residues. Other required measurements, besides d.b.h. and end of utilization, are the top of the sawtimber portion (7.0 inches in softwoods and 9.0 inches in hardwoods). Those measurements allow calculation of the sawtimber and poletimber portion of the growing-stock section.

## Highlights

### Characteristics of Harvested Trees in Virginia

Results of this study identify several key characteristics of trees harvested. Such findings cannot be obtained from a typical field inventory or a forest industry study that supplies product output data only. Information on such characteristics as average d.b.h. by product, average bole length by product, average residual stump height, and average d.o.b. at the end of utilization is vital to a full understanding of the complex nature of removals. Averages discussed in this section are based on the measurement of 2,016 trees, of which 1,086 (54 percent) were softwood and 930 (46 percent) were hardwood.

According to Howell and Becker (2006), softwood and hardwood saw-log volume together accounted for 47 percent of the total product output for the State. The study classified 459 trees as having softwood saw logs averaging 12.3 inches d.b.h. The study classified 55 percent, or 251 trees, as planted softwood saw logs averaging 11.6 inches d.b.h., while natural softwood saw logs averaged 13.2 inches d.b.h. The study classified 401 hardwood trees as having saw logs averaging 14.1 inches d.b.h.

As expected, the d.b.h. of trees measured for pulpwood and composite panels was significantly smaller. Of the 472 softwood pulpwood trees measured, the average d.b.h. was 7.2 inches, while the 373 trees measured for hardwood pulpwood averaged 7.2 inches d.b.h. Sixty-three percent, or 298 trees, of the softwood pulpwood trees were planted averaging 7.1 inches d.b.h. One hundred and fifty-five trees were measured for softwood composite panels and averaged 7.4 inches d.b.h., while hardwood composite panels averaged 8.3 inches d.b.h. Table 2 shows the breakdown of average d.b.h. for each product by species group and stand origin.

Bole length is the distance between a 1-foot stump and a 4-inch top. As expected, trees harvested for solid wood products tended to have longer average bole lengths than trees harvested for pulpwood or composite panel products. The average bole length for softwood trees measured for saw logs was 60 feet, while trees measured for hardwood saw logs had an average bole length of 59 feet. In comparison, trees measured for softwood pulpwood had an average bole length of 33 feet, and hardwood pulpwood had an average bole length of 31 feet. Softwood composite panel trees had an average bole length of 34 feet, while trees measured for hardwood composite panels had an average bole length of 35 feet. Trees measured in planted stands tended to have shorter bole lengths than those measured in the natural stands. Table 3 shows the average bole length by species group and stand origin.

Residual stump height is a key component in determining utilization rates for harvested trees. By FIA standards, the stump is that portion of the tree measured at ground level from the uphill side of the tree to 1 foot up the bole. Loggers try to maximize volume harvested by cutting the tree as close to the ground as possible. Residual stump heights across all products ranged from 0.40 to 0.70 feet;

**Table 2—Average diameter at breast height by species group, stand origin, and product, Virginia, 2007**

| Species group and stand origin | Product | | | |
|---|---|---|---|---|
| | Saw logs | Composite panels | Pulpwood | Fuelwood |
| | *inches* | | | |
| Softwood | | | | |
| Natural | 13.15 | 8.42 | 7.49 | 5.20 |
| Planted | 11.56 | 6.99 | 7.08 | — |
| Total | 12.28 | 7.44 | 7.23 | 5.20 |
| Hardwood | | | | |
| Natural | 14.14 | 8.33 | 7.36 | 6.21 |
| Planted | 12.70 | 7.20 | 6.58 | — |
| Total | 14.14 | 8.25 | 7.21 | 6.21 |

— = no sample for the cell.

**Table 3—Average bole length by species group, stand origin, and product, Virginia, 2007**

| Species group and stand origin | Product | | | |
|---|---|---|---|---|
| | Saw logs | Composite panels | Pulpwood | Fuelwood |
| | *feet* | | | |
| Softwood | | | | |
| Natural | 62.32 | 38.10 | 37.07 | — |
| Planted | 57.78 | 32.34 | 30.76 | — |
| Total | 59.83 | 34.16 | 33.03 | — |
| Hardwood | | | | |
| Natural | 58.97 | 34.40 | 31.42 | 24.31 |
| Planted | 68.00 | 37.17 | 27.96 | — |
| Total | 59.00 | 34.62 | 30.76 | 24.31 |

— = no sample for the cell.

however, most softwood trees harvested had an average residual stump height of about a 0.50 foot, while harvested hardwood trees averaged slightly higher than one-half foot residual stumps. In softwoods and across all products, this accounted for about 46 percent of the stump volume used. In hardwoods and across all products, about 32 percent of stump volume was used. Stump volume for both hardwood and softwood contributed to utilization of the nongrowing-stock portion of trees, i.e., overutilization. Residual stump heights for trees coming from natural stands appear slightly higher than heights coming from planted stands. Table 4 shows the average residual stump heights for each product by species group and stand origin.

The final component we used to determine use rates was d.o.b. at the end of utilization. Tops and limbs constitute most of the nongrowing-stock volume, although they accounted for only 38 percent of the nongrowing-stock portion that was utilized. The average end of utilization for softwood saw logs was 5.3 inches, and for hardwood saw logs 6.1 inches. The average end of utilization for softwood and hardwood pulpwood was 3.3 and 3.9 inches, respectively. Table 5 shows the average end of utilization by the different products, species group and stand origin.

**Table 4—Average residual stump height by species group, stand origin, and product, Virginia, 2007**

| Species group and stand origin | Product | | | |
|---|---|---|---|---|
| | Saw logs | Composite panels | Pulpwood | Fuelwood |
| | *feet* | | | |
| Softwood | | | | |
| Natural | 0.51 | 0.43 | 0.48 | — |
| Planted | 0.46 | 0.48 | 0.46 | — |
| Total | 0.48 | 0.47 | 0.47 | — |
| Hardwood | | | | |
| Natural | 0.60 | 0.70 | 0.55 | 0.52 |
| Planted | 0.40 | 0.50 | 0.51 | — |
| Total | 0.60 | 0.68 | 0.54 | 0.52 |

— = no sample for the cell.

**Table 5—Average end of utilization by species group, stand origin, and product, Virginia, 2007**

| Species group and stand origin | Product | | | |
|---|---|---|---|---|
| | Saw logs | Composite panels | Pulpwood | Fuelwood |
| | *inches* | | | |
| Softwood | | | | |
| Natural | 5.39 | 3.97 | 3.81 | — |
| Planted | 5.24 | 3.56 | 3.07 | — |
| Total | 5.31 | 3.69 | 3.34 | — |
| Hardwood | | | | |
| Natural | 6.11 | 4.58 | 3.92 | 2.90 |
| Planted | 4.00 | 3.88 | 3.81 | — |
| Total | 6.11 | 4.53 | 3.90 | 2.90 |

— = no sample for the cell.

## Softwood Removals

Results from this study document 18,307 cubic feet of softwood volume, of which 15,744 cubic feet, or 86 percent, was used for product(s). Fourteen percent, or 2,563 cubic feet, was left onsite as logging residue (fig. 3). Thirty-one percent of the residue volume came from the growing-stock portion of the tree, while 69 percent came from the nongrowing-stock portion (stumps, tops, and limbs) (fig. 4) (table A.1).

The total softwood growing-stock volume measured was 16,040 cubic feet, of which 95 percent was utilized and 5 percent was logging residue (fig. 5). By FIA

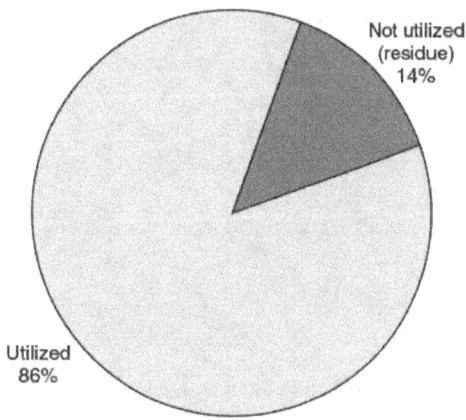

Total 18.3 thousand cubic feet

Figure 3—Disposition of total softwood harvest volume, Virginia, 2007.

merchantability standards, the logging residue portion of growing-stock trees is underutilized volume. Of the total utilized volume, 493 cubic feet, or 3.1 percent was from the nongrowing-stock portion of trees. By the same merchantability standards, that volume is considered overutilization (tables A.2 and A.3).

Softwood volumes and percentages are broken down further by poletimber and sawtimber, and by the various products measured (tables A.2 through A.9). By product, trees harvested for pulpwood had above-average rate of utilization for the merchantable portion of the tree at 97.4 percent and the highest rate of overutilization at 8.4 percent, meaning that more of the nongrowing-stock portion of the tree was being used for product(s) and less was left as logging residue.

Softwood percentages and volumes presented in these tables represent only trees measured in this study of 41 active harvest operations. However, it is possible to apply the percentages to inventory data from Virginia's eighth survey (Rose 2009) to get an estimate of total softwood logging residues for the State. Annual softwood removal from all-live trees was 340.6 million cubic feet. Softwood growing-stock removals were 331.6 million cubic feet, or 97 percent of the total. Applying the factors from this study to total softwood removals for all-live trees tallied in the State survey provides an estimate of 84.3 million cubic feet total annual softwood residue. Of the total residue for all-live trees, 30.6 million cubic feet, or 36 percent, was considered growing-stock residue. The remaining 64 percent, or 53.8 million cubic feet, was nongrowing-stock residue from stumps, tops and limbs, and cull trees not used.

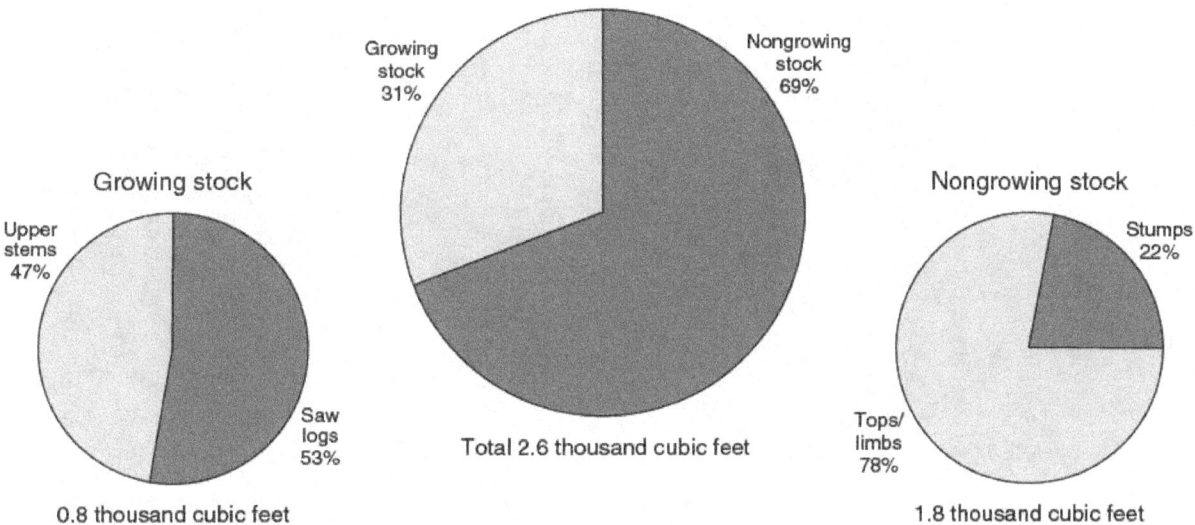

Figure 4—Softwood residue by volume type, Virginia, 2007.

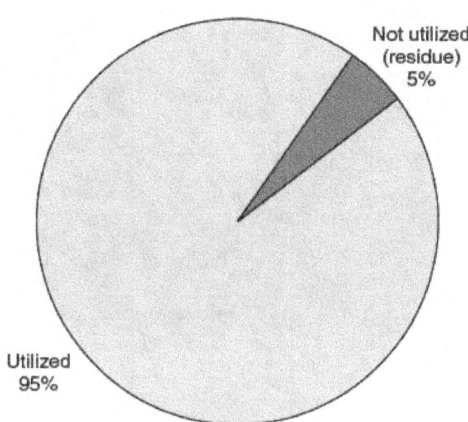

Figure 5—Disposition of softwood growing-stock volume, Virginia, 2007.

## Hardwood Removals

Results from this study document 20,327 cubic feet of hard-wood volume, of which 16,029 cubic feet, or 79 percent, was utilized for product(s). Twenty-one percent, or 4,298 cubic feet, was left onsite as logging residue (fig. 6). Thirty-two percent of residue volume came from the growing-stock portion of trees, and 68 percent came from the nongrowing-stock portion (stumps, tops, and limbs) (fig. 7) (table A.1).

The total hardwood growing-stock volume measured was 16,916 cubic feet, of which 92 percent was used and 8 percent was logging residue (fig. 8). By FIA merchant-ability standards, the logging residue portion is underutilized volume. Of the total utilized volume 499 cubic feet, or 3.1 percent, was from the nongrowing-stock portion of trees. By the same merchantability standards, that volume is considered overutilization (tables A.10 and A.11).

Hardwood volumes and percentages also were measured for poletimber and sawtimber, and differentiated by the various products they provided (tables A.10 through A.17). At 94 percent, however, those trees measured for pulpwood were more fully utilized. More of the nongrowing-stock portion was used for pulpwood and fuelwood. Trees measured for hardwood saw logs and composite panels were the least utilized of all, although they have the most nongrowing-stock material.

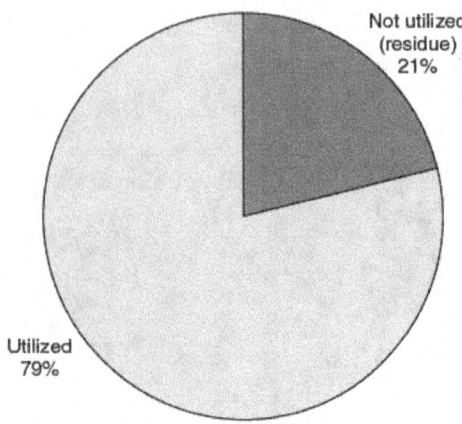

Not utilized (residue) 21%

Utilized 79%

Total 20.3 thousand cubic feet

Figure 6—Disposition of total hardwood harvest volume, Virginia, 2007.

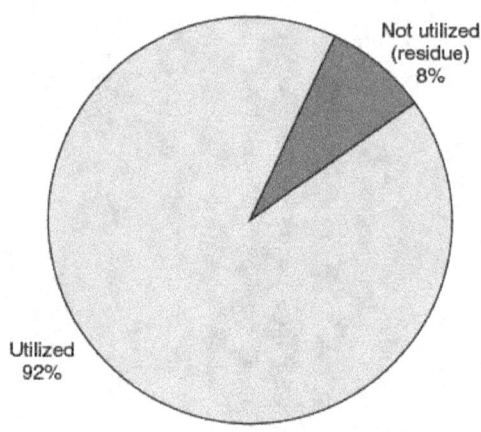

Not utilized (residue) 8%

Utilized 92%

Total 16.9 thousand cubic feet

Figure 8—Disposition of hardwood growing-stock volume, Virginia, 2007.

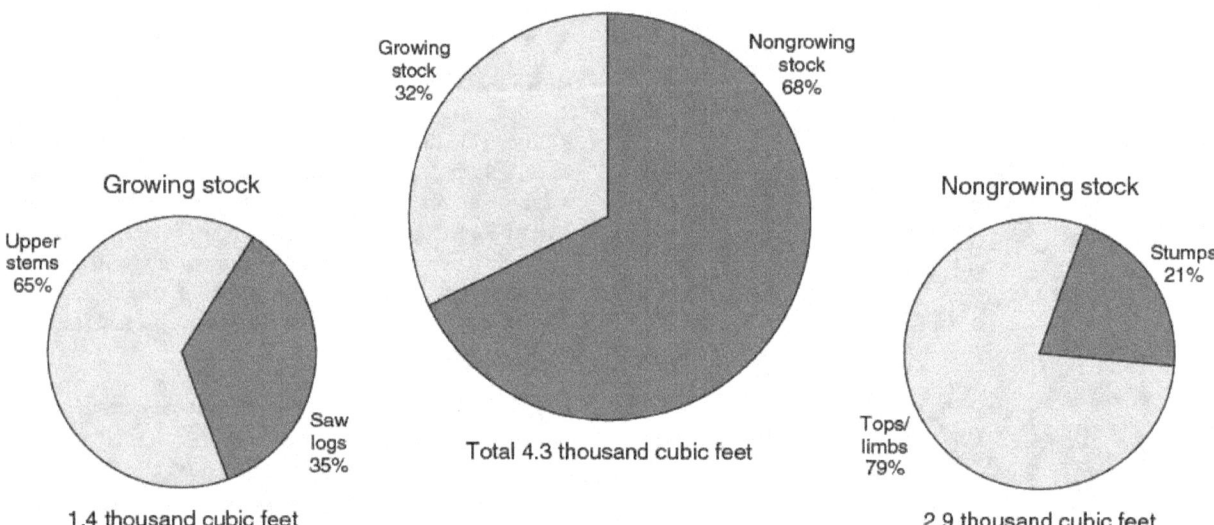

Growing stock 32%

Nongrowing stock 68%

Growing stock

Upper stems 65%

Saw logs 35%

1.4 thousand cubic feet

Total 4.3 thousand cubic feet

Nongrowing stock

Stumps 21%

Tops/ limbs 79%

2.9 thousand cubic feet

Figure 7—Hardwood residue by volume type, Virginia, 2007.

Hardwood percentages and volumes presented in the tables represent only trees measured in this study of 40 active harvest operations. However, it is possible to apply the percentages to inventory data from Virginia's eighth survey (Rose 2009) to provide an estimate of total hardwood logging residue for the State. Annual hardwood removals from all-live trees totaled 487.0 million cubic feet. Hardwood growing-stock removals totaled 442.1 million cubic feet, or 91 percent of that total. Applying factors from this study to total hardwood removals from all-live trees tallied in the State survey provided an estimate of 147.7 million cubic feet total annual hardwood residue. Of that total, 72.0 million cubic feet, or 49 percent, was considered growing-stock residue. The remaining 51 percent, or 75.7 million cubic feet, was nongrowing-stock residue from stumps, tops and limbs, and rough or rotten trees that were not used.

## Virginia's Potential Biomass Availability

Logging residue has long been viewed as a possible source for bioenergy and other timber products, although traditionally it has not had any merchantable value. Retrieval of logging residue is a matter of economics, based on markets or demand. If markets are available and a willingness to pay a reasonable price exists, then more total tree volume is utilized for products. With this in mind, logging residue volume in Virginia for 2002–2007, or the eighth survey, amounted to 232.0 million cubic feet, or 8.5 million green tons. Nearly 148 million cubic feet (5.7 million tons), or 64 percent, of the logging residues generated came from hardwoods, while 84.3 million cubic feet (2.9 million tons) came from softwood species. Logging residue from the merchantable portion of all-live tree removals totaled 102.5 million cubic feet (3.8 million tons), or 44 percent of the total logging residue. Other sources accounted for 129.4 million cubic feet (4.7 million tons), or 56 percent of the total logging residue. Trees < 5 inches d.b.h. contributed another 2.2 million tons of possible logging residue. Tables 6 and 7 express the volume of timber removals by removals class, species group, and source in million cubic feet and green tons.

Over the same period, the area of timber harvested annually in Virginia amounted to 319,600 acres, of which 133,600 acres (42 percent) underwent a final harvest, while 117,900 acres (37 percent) had a partial harvest, and 55,000 acres (17 percent) had commercial thinning. The removals volume attributed to timber products and logging residues are directly related to these treated acres. Based on the treated acres, an estimated 86.5 tons per acre in the merchantable and nonmerchantable portion of trees > 5 inches d.b.h. were removed annually from Virginia's timberland. Of the nearly 87 tons removed, 59.8 tons per acre were utilized for products, while 24.0 tons per acre were left as logging residue, excluding the residual stump. Assuming a 20-percent recovery rate for trees < 5 inches d.b.h., an additional 1.4 tons per acre was added bringing the total logging residue to 25.4 tons per acre. This volume of logging residue is equivalent to about one tree-length trailer load of wood for every acre treated in Virginia.

**Table 6—Volume of timber removals by removals class, species group, and source, Virginia, 2007**

| Removals class and species group | All sources | Source |  |
|---|---|---|---|
|  |  | All live removals | Other sources |
|  | *million cubic feet* | | |
| **Roundwood products** | | | |
| Softwood | 262.0 | 250.7 | 11.4 |
| Hardwood | 265.1 | 257.2 | 8.0 |
| Total | 527.2 | 507.8 | 19.3 |
| **Logging residues** | | | |
| Softwood | 84.3 | 30.6 | 53.8 |
| Hardwood | 147.7 | 72.0 | 75.7 |
| Total | 232.0 | 102.5 | 129.4 |
| **Other removals** | | | |
| Softwood | 73.1 | 59.4 | 13.7 |
| Hardwood | 197.9 | 157.8 | 40.1 |
| Total | 271.0 | 217.2 | 53.8 |
| **Total removals** | | | |
| Softwood | 419.5 | 340.6 | 78.9 |
| Hardwood | 610.7 | 487.0 | 123.7 |
| Total | 1,030.2 | 827.6 | 202.6 |

Numbers in rows and columns may not sum to totals due to rounding.

**Table 7—Volume of timber removals by removals class, species group, and source, Virginia, 2007**

| Removals class and species group | All sources | Source | |
|---|---|---|---|
| | | All live removals | Other sources |
| | *green tons* | | |
| **Roundwood products** | | | |
| Softwood | 8,963,294 | 8,574,166 | 389,128 |
| Hardwood | 10,145,675 | 9,841,310 | 304,365 |
| Total | 19,108,969 | 18,415,476 | 693,493 |
| **Logging residues** | | | |
| Softwood | 2,884,395 | 1,045,068 | 1,839,327 |
| Hardwood | 5,650,472 | 2,754,984 | 2,895,488 |
| Total | 8,534,867 | 3,800,052 | 4,734,815 |
| **Other removals** | | | |
| Softwood | 2,500,438 | 2,030,139 | 470,299 |
| Hardwood | 7,572,833 | 6,038,800 | 1,534,033 |
| Total | 10,073,271 | 8,068,939 | 2,004,332 |
| **Total removals** | | | |
| Softwood | 14,348,127 | 11,649,373 | 2,698,754 |
| Hardwood | 23,368,980 | 18,635,094 | 4,733,886 |
| Total | 37,717,107 | 30,284,467 | 7,432,640 |

Most loggers are very well equipped to handle the main bole or merchantable portion of the tree and even long straight sections of forks or major limbs. However, a more effective way to handle rough trees with crooked boles, tops, and limbs is to chip this material at the site and transport the material in chip vans. Whole trees and portions of trees chipped on site have a very limited use for industrial timber products. About the only use for this material is as mulch or boiler fuel. Bioenergy and mulch markets are particularly cost-efficient means of dealing with small trees < 5 inches d.b.h. as well as with rough and rotten trees and the nonmerchantable portions of growing-stock trees. With conventional logging equipment, a 60-percent recovery rate is a realistic goal for possible extraction of formerly unutilized material (Perlack and others 2005). At this recovery rate an additional 15.2 tons per acre of material once classified as logging residue could be added to the volume going for timber products.

## Literature Cited

Bechtold, W.A.; Patterson, P.L., eds. 2005. The enhanced forest inventory and analysis program—national sampling design and estimation procedures. Gen. Tech. Rep. SRS–80. Asheville, NC: U.S. Department of Agriculture Forest Service, Southern Research Station. 85 p.

Howell, M.; Becker, C.W. 2006. Virginia's timber industry—an assessment of timber product output and use, 2003. Resour. Bull. SRS–108. Asheville, NC: U.S. Department of Agriculture Forest Service, Southern Research Station. 44 p.

Perlack, R.D.; Wright, L.L.; Turhollow, A. [and others]. 2005. Biomass as feedstock for a bioenergy and bioproducts industry: the technical feasibility of a billion-ton annual supply. ORNL/TM-2005/66. Washington DC: U.S. Department of Energy and U.S. Department of Agriculture Forest Service. 73 p.

Rose, A.K. 2009. Virginia's forests, 2007. Resour. Bull. SRS–159. Asheville, NC: U.S. Department of Agriculture Forest Service, Southern Research Station. 77 p.

# Glossary

**Board foot.** Unit of measure applied to roundwood. It relates to lumber that is 1-foot long, 1-foot wide, and 1-inch thick (or its equivalent).

**Composite products.** Roundwood products manufactured into chips, wafers, strands, flakes, shavings, or sawdust and then reconstituted into a variety of panel and engineered lumber products.

**Drain.** The volume of roundwood removed from any geographic area where timber is grown.

**Growing-stock removals.** The growing-stock volume removed from poletimber and sawtimber trees in the timberland inventory. (Note: Includes volume removed for roundwood products, logging residues, and other removals.)

**Growing-stock trees.** Living trees of commercial species classified as sawtimber, poletimber, saplings, and seedlings. Growing-stock trees must contain at least one 12-foot or two 8-foot logs in the saw-log portion, currently or potentially (if too small to qualify). The log(s) must meet dimension and merchantability standards and have, currently or potentially, one-third of the gross board-foot volume in sound wood.

**Growing-stock volume.** The cubic-foot volume of sound wood in growing-stock trees at least 5.0 inches d.b.h. from a 1-foot stump to a minimum 4.0-inch top d.o.b. of the central stem.

**Hardwoods.** Dicotyledonous trees, usually broadleaf and deciduous.

> *Soft hardwoods.* Hardwood species with an average specific gravity of 0.50 or less, such as gums, yellow-poplar, cottonwoods, red maple, basswoods, and willows.

> *Hard hardwoods.* Hardwood species with an average specific gravity > 0.50, such as oaks, hard maples, hickories, and beech.

**Industrial roundwood products.** Any primary use of the main stem of a tree, such as saw logs, pulpwood, and veneer logs, intended to be processed into primary wood products, such as lumber, wood pulp, and sheathing, at primary wood-using mills.

**International ¼-inch rule.** A log rule or formula for estimating the board-foot volume of logs, allowing ½-inch of taper for each 4-foot length. The rule appears in a number of forms that allow for kerf. In the form used by FIA, a ¼-inch of kerf is assumed. This rule is used as the USDA Forest Service standard log rule in the Eastern United States.

**Log.** A primary forest product harvested in long, primarily 8-, 12-, and 16-foot lengths.

**Logging residues.** The unused portion of trees cut or destroyed during logging operations.

**Merchantable portion.** That portion of live trees 5.0 inches d.b.h. and larger between a 1-foot stump and a minimum 4.0-inch top d.o.b. on the central stem. That portion of primary forks from the point of occurrence to a minimum 4.0-inch top d.o.b. is included.

**Merchantable volume.** Solid-wood volume in the merchantable portion of live trees.

**Noncommercial species.** Tree species of typically small size, poor form, or inferior quality that normally do not develop into trees suitable for industrial wood products.

**Nonforest land.** Land that has never supported forests and land formerly forested where timber production is precluded by development for other uses.

**Nongrowing-stock sources.** The net volume removed from the nongrowing-stock portions of poletimber and sawtimber trees (stumps, tops, limbs, cull sections of central stem) and from any portion of a rough, rotten, sapling, dead, or nonforest tree.

**Other forest land.** Forest land other than timberland and productive reserved forest land. It includes available and reserved forest land that is incapable of producing annually 20 cubic feet per acre of industrial wood under natural conditions because of adverse site conditions such as sterile soils, dry climate, poor drainage, high elevation, steepness, or rockiness.

**Other products.** A miscellaneous category of roundwood products, e.g., cooperage, excelsior, shingles, and mill residue byproducts (charcoal, bedding, mulch, etc.).

**Other removals.** The growing-stock volume of trees removed from the inventory by cultural operations such as timber stand improvement, land clearing, and other changes in land use, resulting in the removal of the trees from timberland.

**Other sources.** (See: Nongrowing-stock sources.)

**Poletimber-size trees.** Softwoods 5.0 to 8.9 inches d.b.h. and hardwoods 5.0 to 10.9 inches d.b.h.

**Posts, poles, and pilings.** Roundwood products milled (cut or peeled) into standard sizes (lengths and circumferences) to be put in the ground to provide vertical and lateral support in buildings, foundations, utility lines, and fences. May also include nonindustrial (unmilled) products.

**Primary wood-using plants.** Industries that convert roundwood products (saw logs, veneer logs, pulpwood, etc.) into primary wood products, such as lumber, veneer or sheathing, and wood pulp.

**Pulpwood.** A roundwood product that will be reduced to individual wood fibers by chemical or mechanical means. The fibers are used to make a broad generic group of pulp products that includes paper products, as well as chipboard, fiberboard, insulating board, and paperboard.

**Rotten trees.** Live trees of commercial species not containing at least one 12-foot saw log, or two noncontiguous saw logs, each 8 feet or longer, now or prospectively, primarily because of rot or missing sections, and with less than one-third of the gross board-foot tree volume in sound material.

**Rough trees.** Live trees of commercial species not containing at least one 12-foot saw log, or two noncontiguous saw logs, each 8 feet or longer, now or prospectively, primarily because of roughness, poor form, splits, and cracks, and with less than one-third of the gross board-foot tree volume in sound material; and live trees of noncommercial species.

**Roundwood (roundwood logs).** Logs, bolts, or other round sections cut from trees for industrial manufacture or consumer uses.

**Roundwood chipped.** Any timber cut primarily for industrial manufacture, delivered to nonpulpmills, chipped, and then sold to pulpmills for use as fiber. Includes tops, jump sections, whole trees, and pulpwood sticks.

**Roundwood product drain.** That portion of total drain used for a product.

**Roundwood products.** Any primary product, such as lumber, poles, pilings, pulp, or fuelwood that is produced from roundwood.

**Salvable dead trees.** Standing or downed dead trees that were formerly growing stock and considered merchantable. Trees must be at least 5.0 inches d.b.h. to qualify.

**Saplings.** Live trees 1.0 to 5.0 inches d.b.h.

**Saw log.** A roundwood product, usually 8 feet in length or longer, processed into a variety of sawn products such as lumber, cants, pallets, railroad ties, and timbers.

**Saw-log portion.** The part of the bole of sawtimber trees between a 1-foot stump and the saw-log top.

**Saw-log top.** The point on the bole of sawtimber trees above which a conventional saw log cannot be produced. The minimum saw-log top is 7.0 inches d.o.b. for softwoods and 9.0 inches d.o.b. for hardwoods.

**Sawtimber-size trees.** Softwoods 9.0 inches d.b.h. and larger and hardwoods 11.0 inches d.b.h. and larger.

**Sawtimber volume.** Growing-stock volume in the saw-log portion of sawtimber-sized trees in board feet (International ¼-inch rule).

**Seedlings.** Trees <1.0 inch d.b.h. and >1 foot tall for hardwoods, >6 inches tall for softwood, and >0.5 inch in diameter at ground level for longleaf pine.

**Softwoods.** Coniferous trees, usually evergreen, having leaves that are needles or scalelike.

**Standard cord.** A unit of measure applied to roundwood, usually bolts or split wood. It is a stack of wood 4 feet high, 4 feet wide, and 8 feet long encompassing 128 cubic feet of wood, bark, and air space. This usually translates to approximately 75.0 to 81.0 cubic feet of solid wood for pulpwood, because pulpwood is more uniform.

**Standard unit.** A unit measure applied to roundwood timber products. Board feet (International ¼-inch rule) is the standard unit used for saw logs and veneer; cords are used for pulpwood, composite panel, and fuelwood; hundred pieces for poles; thousand pieces for posts; and thousand cubic feet for all other miscellaneous forest products.

**Timberland.** Forest land capable of producing 20 cubic feet of industrial wood per acre per year and not withdrawn from timber utilization.

**Timber product output.** The total volume of roundwood products from all sources plus the volume of byproducts recovered from mill residues (equals roundwood product drain).

**Timber products.** Roundwood products and byproducts.

**Timber removals.** The total volume of trees removed from the timberland inventory by harvesting, cultural operations such as stand improvement, land clearing, or changes in land use. (Note: Includes roundwood products, logging residues, and other removals.)

**Tree.** Woody plant having one erect perennial stem or trunk at least 3 inches d.b.h., a more or less definitely formed crown of foliage, and a height of at least 13 feet (at maturity).

**Upper-stem portion.** The part of the main stem of sawtimber trees above the saw-log top and the minimum top diameter of 4.0 inches outside bark, or to the point where the main stem breaks into limbs.

**Utilization studies.** Studies conducted on active logging operations to develop factors for merchantable portions of trees left in the woods (logging residues), logging damage, and utilization of the unmerchantable portion of growing-stock trees and nongrowing-stock trees.

**Veneer log.** A roundwood product either rotary cut, sliced, stamped, or sawn into a variety of veneer products such as plywood, finished panels, veneer sheets, or sheathing.

**Weight.** A unit of measure for mill residues, expressed as oven-dry tons (2,000 oven-dry pounds).

# Appendix

## Index of Tables

**Table A.1—Harvest and utilization volume by species group, source, and volume type, Virginia, 2007**

| Species group and source | Total tree volume | Growing stock | | | | | | Nongrowing stock | | | | |
|---|---|---|---|---|---|---|---|---|---|---|---|---|
| | | Total | Saw log | | Upper stem | | Total | Stumps | | Tops/limbs | | |
| | | | Utilized | Not utilized | Utilized | Not utilized | | Utilized | Not utilized | Utilized | Not utilized | |
| | | | | | | *cubic feet* | | | | | | |
| Softwood | | | | | | | | | | | | |
| Sawtimber | 15,531.61 | 13,755.34 | 12,130.03 | 416.04 | 853.61 | 355.66 | 1,776.27 | 258.66 | 312.11 | 22.31 | 1,183.19 | |
| Poletimber | 2,774.98 | 2,285.01 | — | — | 2,267.05 | 17.96 | 489.97 | 70.56 | 77.53 | 141.52 | 200.36 | |
| Total | 18,306.59 | 16,040.35 | 12,130.03 | 416.04 | 3,120.66 | 373.62 | 2,266.24 | 329.22 | 389.64 | 163.83 | 1,383.55 | |
| Hardwood | | | | | | | | | | | | |
| Sawtimber | 17,093.27 | 14,315.05 | 11,821.32 | 491.91 | 1,184.48 | 817.34 | 2,778.22 | 207.05 | 488.15 | 113.97 | 1,969.05 | |
| Poletimber | 3,233.91 | 2,600.53 | — | — | 2,523.99 | 76.54 | 633.38 | 74.48 | 121.42 | 103.53 | 333.95 | |
| Total | 20,327.18 | 16,915.58 | 11,821.32 | 491.91 | 3,708.47 | 893.88 | 3,411.60 | 281.53 | 609.57 | 217.50 | 2,303.00 | |

Numbers in rows and columns may not sum to totals due to rounding.

— = no sample for the cell.


**Table A.2—Volume of softwood growing stock by product and utilization for sawtimber and poletimber, Virginia, 2007**

| Product | Total volume utilized | Growing stock | | | Nongrowing stock utilized | Saw-log portion | | | |
|---|---|---|---|---|---|---|---|---|---|
| | | Total | Utilized | Not utilized | | Total | Utilized | Cull utilized | Not utilized |
| | | | | | *cubic feet* | | | | |
| Saw logs | 12,952.94 | 13,392.99 | 12,682.74 | 710.25 | 270.20 | 11,882.11 | 11,505.26 | 369.50 | 7.35 |
| Veneer logs | — | — | — | — | — | — | — | — | — |
| Composite panels | 228.43 | 235.73 | 219.76 | 15.97 | 8.67 | 133.86 | 122.80 | 9.87 | 1.19 |
| Pulpwood | 2,562.37 | 2,411.65 | 2,348.21 | 63.44 | 214.16 | 530.10 | 501.97 | 26.09 | 2.04 |
| Fuelwood | — | — | — | — | — | — | — | — | — |
| Total | 15,743.74 | 16,040.37 | 15,250.71 | 789.66 | 493.03 | 12,546.07 | 12,130.03 | 405.46 | 10.58 |

Numbers in rows and columns may not sum to totals due to rounding.

— = no sample for the cell.

**Table A.3—Percent of overutilization and underutilization for softwood growing stock by product for sawtimber and poletimber, Virginia, 2007**

| | Overutilization | | Underutilization | | Saw-log portion | | |
|---|---|---|---|---|---|---|---|
| Product | Growing stock utilized/ total volume utilized | Nongrowing stock utilized/ total volume utilized | Growing stock utilized/ total growing-stock volume | Growing stock not utilized/ total growing-stock volume | Saw log utilized/ total saw-log volume | Cull utilized/ total saw-log volume | Saw log not utilized/ total saw-log volume |
| | *percent* | | | | | | |
| Saw logs | 97.91 | 2.09 | 94.70 | 5.30 | 96.83 | 3.11 | 0.06 |
| Veneer logs | — | — | — | — | — | — | — |
| Composite panels | 96.20 | 3.80 | 93.23 | 6.77 | 91.74 | 7.37 | — |
| Pulpwood | 91.64 | 8.36 | 97.37 | 2.63 | 94.69 | 4.92 | — |
| Fuelwood | — | — | — | — | — | — | — |
| All products | 96.87 | 3.13 | 95.08 | 4.92 | 96.68 | 3.23 | 0.08 |

— = no sample for the cell.

**Table A.4—Volume of softwood growing stock by product and utilization for sawtimber, Virginia, 2007**

| | | Growing stock | | | | Saw-log portion | | | |
|---|---|---|---|---|---|---|---|---|---|
| Product | Total volume utilized | Total | Utilized | Not utilized | Nongrowing stock utilized | Total | Utilized | Cull utilized | Not utilized |
| | *cubic feet* | | | | | | | | |
| Saw logs | 12,459.14 | 12,915.62 | 12,207.96 | 707.66 | 251.18 | 11,882.11 | 11,505.26 | 369.50 | 7.35 |
| Veneer logs | — | — | — | — | — | — | — | — | — |
| Composite panels | 148.97 | 160.29 | 145.03 | 15.26 | 3.94 | 133.86 | 122.80 | 9.87 | 1.19 |
| Pulpwood | 656.50 | 679.44 | 630.66 | 48.78 | 25.84 | 530.10 | 501.97 | 26.09 | 2.04 |
| Fuelwood | — | — | — | — | — | — | — | — | — |
| Total | 13,264.61 | 13,755.35 | 12,983.65 | 771.70 | 280.96 | 12,546.07 | 12,130.03 | 405.46 | 10.58 |

Numbers in rows and columns may not sum to totals due to rounding.

— = no sample for the cell.

**Table A.5—Percent of overutilization and underutilization for softwood growing stock by product for sawtimber, Virginia, 2007**

| Product | Overutilization | | Underutilization | | Saw-log portion | | |
| --- | --- | --- | --- | --- | --- | --- | --- |
| | Growing stock utilized/ total volume utilized | Nongrowing stock utilized/ total volume utilized | Growing stock utilized/ total growing-stock volume | Growing stock not utilized/ total growing-stock volume | Saw log utilized/ total saw-log volume | Cull utilized/ total saw-log volume | Saw log not utilized/ total saw-log volume |
| | *percent* | | | | | | |
| Saw logs | 97.98 | 2.02 | 94.52 | 5.48 | 96.83 | 3.11 | 0.06 |
| Veneer logs | — | — | — | — | — | — | — |
| Composite panels | 97.36 | 2.64 | 90.48 | 9.52 | 91.74 | 7.37 | — |
| Pulpwood | 96.06 | 3.94 | 92.82 | 7.18 | 94.69 | 4.92 | — |
| Fuelwood | — | — | — | — | — | — | — |
| All products | 97.88 | 2.12 | 94.39 | 5.61 | 96.68 | 3.23 | 0.08 |

— = no sample for the cell.

**Table A.6—Volume of softwood growing stock by product and utilization for poletimber, Virginia, 2007**

| Product | Total volume utilized | Growing stock | | | Nongrowing stock utilized |
| --- | --- | --- | --- | --- | --- |
| | | Total | Utilized | Not utilized | |
| | *cubic feet* | | | | |
| Saw logs | 493.80 | 477.37 | 474.78 | 2.59 | 19.02 |
| Veneer logs | — | — | — | — | — |
| Composite panels | 79.46 | 75.44 | 74.73 | 0.71 | 4.73 |
| Pulpwood | 1,905.87 | 1,732.21 | 1,717.55 | 14.66 | 188.32 |
| Fuelwood | — | — | — | — | — |
| Total | 2,479.13 | 2,285.02 | 2,267.06 | 17.96 | 212.07 |

Numbers in rows and columns may not sum to totals due to rounding.

— = no sample for the cell.

**Table A.7—Percent of overutilization and underutilization for softwood growing stock by product for poletimber, Virginia, 2007**

| | Overutilization | | Underutilization | |
| --- | --- | --- | --- | --- |
| Product | Growing stock utilized/ total volume utilized | Nongrowing stock utilized/ total volume utilized | Growing stock utilized/ total growing-stock volume | Growing stock not utilized/ total growing-stock volume |
| | *percent* | | | |
| Saw logs | 96.15 | 3.85 | 99.46 | 0.54 |
| Veneer logs | — | — | — | — |
| Composite panels | 94.05 | 5.95 | 99.06 | 0.94 |
| Pulpwood | 90.12 | 9.88 | 99.15 | 0.85 |
| Fuelwood | — | — | — | — |
| All products | 91.45 | 8.55 | 99.21 | 0.79 |

— = no sample for the cell.

**Table A.8—Volume of softwood cull by product and utilization, Virginia, 2007**

| | | Nongrowing stock | | | |
| --- | --- | --- | --- | --- | --- |
| | | Merchantable | | | |
| Product | Total volume utilized | Total | Utilized | Not utilized | Unmerchantable utilized |
| | | *cubic feet* | | | |
| Saw logs | 15.12 | 14.62 | 14.62 | — | 0.50 |
| Veneer logs | — | — | — | — | — |
| Composite panels | 875.70 | 817.42 | 811.46 | 5.96 | 64.24 |
| Pulpwood | 621.02 | 581.98 | 580.28 | 1.70 | 40.74 |
| Fuelwood | — | — | — | — | — |
| Total | 1,511.84 | 1,414.02 | 1,406.36 | 7.66 | 105.48 |

Numbers in rows and columns may not sum to totals due to rounding.

— = no sample for the cell.

**Table A.9—Percent of overutilization and underutilization for softwood cull by product, Virginia, 2007**

| | Overutilization | | Underutilization | |
|---|---|---|---|---|
| Product | Merchantable utilized/ total volume utilized | Unmerchantable utilized/ total volume utilized | Merchantable utilized/total merchantable volume | Merchantable not utilized/total merchantable volume |
| | *percent* | | | |
| Saw logs | 96.69 | 3.31 | 100.00 | — |
| Veneer logs | — | — | — | — |
| Composite panels | 92.66 | 7.34 | 99.27 | — |
| Pulpwood | 93.44 | 6.56 | 99.71 | 0.29 |
| Fuelwood | — | — | — | — |
| All products | 93.02 | 6.98 | 99.46 | 0.54 |

— = no sample for the cell.

**Table A.10—Volume of hardwood growing stock by product and utilization for sawtimber and poletimber, Virginia, 2007**

| | | Growing stock | | | | Saw-log portion | | | |
|---|---|---|---|---|---|---|---|---|---|
| Product | Total volume utilized | Total | Utilized | Not utilized | Nongrowing stock utilized | Total | Utilized | Cull utilized | Not utilized |
| | *cubic feet* | | | | | | | | |
| Saw logs | 13,994.34 | 14,905.88 | 13,647.22 | 1,258.66 | 347.12 | 11,943.61 | 11,506.01 | 258.65 | 178.95 |
| Veneer logs | — | — | — | — | — | — | — | — | — |
| Composite panels | 54.79 | 60.98 | 54.50 | 6.48 | 0.29 | 10.44 | 8.37 | 2.07 | — |
| Pulpwood | 1,813.44 | 1,795.79 | 1,687.46 | 108.33 | 125.98 | 347.29 | 296.09 | 51.20 | — |
| Fuelwood | 166.25 | 152.93 | 140.60 | 12.33 | 25.65 | 11.89 | 10.84 | 1.05 | — |
| Total | 16,028.82 | 16,915.58 | 15,529.78 | 1,385.80 | 499.04 | 12,313.23 | 11,821.31 | 312.97 | 178.95 |

Numbers in rows and columns may not sum to totals due to rounding.
— = no sample for the cell.

**Table A.11—Percent of overutilization and underutilization for hardwood growing stock by product for sawtimber and poletimber, Virginia, 2007**

| Product | Overutilization | | Underutilization | | Saw-log portion | | |
|---|---|---|---|---|---|---|---|
| | Growing stock utilized/ total volume utilized | Nongrowing stock utilized/ total volume utilized | Growing stock utilized/ total growing-stock volume | Growing stock not utilized/ total growing-stock volume | Saw log utilized/ total saw-log volume | Cull utilized/ total saw-log volume | Saw log not utilized/ total saw-log volume |
| | | | | *percent* | | | |
| Saw logs | 97.52 | 2.48 | 91.56 | 8.44 | 96.34 | 2.17 | 1.50 |
| Veneer logs | — | — | — | — | — | — | — |
| Composite panels | 99.47 | 0.53 | 89.37 | 10.63 | 80.17 | 19.83 | — |
| Pulpwood | 93.05 | 6.95 | 93.97 | 6.03 | 85.26 | 14.74 | — |
| Fuelwood | 84.57 | 15.43 | 91.94 | 8.06 | 91.17 | 8.83 | — |
| All products | 96.89 | 3.11 | 91.81 | 8.19 | 96.00 | 2.54 | 1.45 |

— = no sample for the cell.

**Table A.12—Volume of hardwood growing stock by product and utilization for sawtimber, Virginia, 2007**

| Product | Total volume utilized | Growing stock | | | Nongrowing stock utilized | Saw-log portion | | | |
|---|---|---|---|---|---|---|---|---|---|
| | | Total | Utilized | Not utilized | | Total | Utilized | Cull utilized | Not utilized |
| | | | | | *cubic feet* | | | | |
| Saw logs | 12,961.23 | 13,887.47 | 12,651.30 | 1,236.17 | 309.93 | 11,943.61 | 11,506.01 | 258.65 | 178.95 |
| Veneer logs | — | — | — | — | — | — | — | — | — |
| Composite panels | 10.12 | 15.00 | 10.04 | 4.96 | 0.08 | 10.44 | 8.37 | 2.07 | — |
| Pulpwood | 337.33 | 394.56 | 327.48 | 67.08 | 9.85 | 347.29 | 296.09 | 51.20 | — |
| Fuelwood | 18.14 | 18.03 | 16.98 | 1.05 | 1.16 | 11.89 | 10.84 | 1.05 | — |
| Total | 13,326.82 | 14,315.06 | 13,005.80 | 1,309.26 | 321.02 | 12,313.23 | 11,821.31 | 312.97 | 178.95 |

Numbers in rows and columns may not sum to totals due to rounding.

— = no sample for the cell.

**Table A.13—Percent of overutilization and underutilization for hardwood growing stock by product for sawtimber, Virginia, 2007**

| Product | Overutilization | | Underutilization | | Saw-log portion | | |
| --- | --- | --- | --- | --- | --- | --- | --- |
| | Growing stock utilized/ total volume utilized | Nongrowing stock utilized/ total volume utilized | Growing stock utilized/ total growing-stock volume | Growing stock not utilized/ total growing-stock volume | Saw log utilized/ total saw-log volume | Cull utilized/ total saw-log volume | Saw log not utilized/ total saw-log volume |
| | _percent_ | | | | | | |
| Saw logs | 97.61 | 2.39 | 91.10 | 8.90 | 96.34 | 2.17 | 1.50 |
| Veneer logs | — | — | — | — | — | — | — |
| Composite panels | — | — | — | — | — | — | — |
| Pulpwood | 97.08 | 2.92 | 83.00 | 17.00 | 85.26 | 14.74 | — |
| Fuelwood | 93.61 | 6.39 | 94.18 | 5.82 | 91.17 | 8.83 | — |
| All products | 97.59 | 2.41 | 90.85 | 9.15 | 96.00 | 2.54 | 1.45 |

— = no sample for the cell.

**Table A.14—Volume of hardwood growing stock by product and utilization for poletimber, Virginia, 2007**

| Product | Total volume utilized | Growing stock | | | Nongrowing stock utilized |
| --- | --- | --- | --- | --- | --- |
| | | Total | Utilized | Not utilized | |
| | _cubic feet_ | | | | |
| Saw logs | 1,033.11 | 1,018.41 | 995.92 | 22.49 | 37.19 |
| Veneer logs | — | — | — | — | — |
| Composite panels | 44.67 | 45.98 | 44.46 | 1.52 | 0.21 |
| Pulpwood | 1,476.11 | 1,401.23 | 1,359.98 | 41.25 | 116.13 |
| Fuelwood | 148.11 | 134.90 | 123.62 | 11.28 | 24.49 |
| Total | 2,702.00 | 2,600.52 | 2,523.98 | 76.54 | 178.02 |

Numbers in rows and columns may not sum to totals due to rounding.

— = no sample for the cell.

**Table A.15—Percent of overutilization and underutilization for hardwood growing stock by product for poletimber, Virginia, 2007**

| Product | Overutilization | | Underutilization | |
|---|---|---|---|---|
| | Growing stock utilized/ total volume utilized | Nongrowing stock utilized/ total volume utilized | Growing stock utilized/ total growing-stock volume | Growing stock not utilized/ total growing-stock volume |
| | *percent* | | | |
| Saw logs | 96.40 | 3.60 | 97.79 | 2.21 |
| Veneer logs | — | — | — | — |
| Composite panels | 99.53 | 0.47 | 96.69 | — |
| Pulpwood | 92.13 | 7.87 | 97.06 | 2.94 |
| Fuelwood | 83.46 | 16.54 | 91.64 | 8.36 |
| All products | 93.41 | 6.59 | 97.06 | 2.94 |

— = no sample for the cell.

**Table A.16—Volume of hardwood cull by product and utilization, Virginia, 2007**

| Product | Total volume utilized | Nongrowing stock | | | Unmerchantable utilized |
|---|---|---|---|---|---|
| | | Merchantable | | | |
| | | Total | Utilized | Not utilized | |
| | | *cubic feet* | | | |
| Saw logs | 219.98 | 215.83 | 215.67 | 0.16 | 4.31 |
| Veneer logs | — | — | — | — | — |
| Composite panels | 600.66 | 600.47 | 580.22 | 20.25 | 20.44 |
| Pulpwood | 972.57 | 929.48 | 905.13 | 24.35 | 67.44 |
| Fuelwood | 50.65 | 43.39 | 41.62 | 1.77 | 9.03 |
| Total | 1,843.86 | 1,789.17 | 1,742.64 | 46.53 | 101.22 |

Numbers in rows and columns may not sum to totals due to rounding.
— = no sample for the cell.

**Table A.17—Percent of overutilization and underutilization for hardwood cull by product, Virginia, 2007**

| Product | Overutilization | | Underutilization | |
|---|---|---|---|---|
| | Merchantable utilized/ total volume utilized | Unmerchantable utilized/ total volume utilized | Merchantable utilized/total merchantable volume | Merchantable not utilized/total merchantable volume |
| | *percent* | | | |
| Saw logs | 98.04 | 1.96 | 99.93 | — |
| Veneer logs | — | — | — | — |
| Composite panels | 96.60 | 3.40 | 96.63 | 3.37 |
| Pulpwood | 93.07 | 6.93 | 97.38 | 2.62 |
| Fuelwood | 82.17 | 17.83 | 95.92 | 4.08 |
| All products | 94.51 | 5.49 | 97.40 | 2.60 |

— = no sample for the cell.